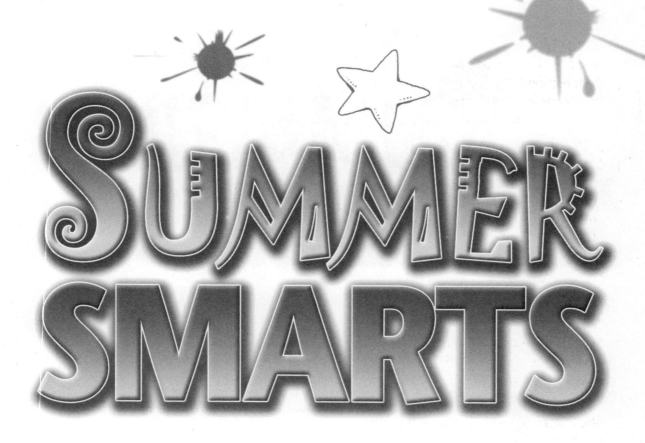

SUMMER SMARTS

Activities in Math, Science, Language Arts, and Social Studies to prepare Students for 3rd Grade

JEANNE CRANE CASTAFERO AND JANET VAN RODEN

KINGFISHER

www.houghtonmifflinbooks.com

Printed in India

ISBN: 978-0-7534-6113-6 (Kingfisher)
ISBN: 0-669-46703-0 (Great Source)

Design: Brown Publishing Network, Inc., Diana Maloney
Design Production: Brown Publishing Network, Inc., Camille Venti

Art: Lynn Jeffery: pages 2, 3, 4, 5, 27, 34, 35, 46 (left), 56 (left), 57, 59, 60, 61, 68, 69, 86, 87, 88. **Joni Levy Liberman:** pages 15, 21, 29 (bottom), 30 (top), 31 (top), 38, 56 (right), 63 (right), 72 (top), 73, 82. **John Magine:** pages 10, 11, 12, 22, 28, 29, 39, 47, 48, 62, 64, 78, 79, 80, 81. **Laura Rader:** 17, 18, 23, 24, 25 (top), 30, 37, 41, 51, 52, 58, 66, 67, 70, 75, 76, 77. **Nadine B. Westcott:** pages 14, 16, 30 (bottom), 31 (bottom), 32, 43, 44, 50, 53, 54, 55, 63 (left), 71, 72 (bottom), 74, 83, 84.

Contents

BOOK SECTION

Who Am I?

What is your **full** name? (first, middle, last)

_____

Do you have a **nickname**? If so, write it below.

_____

Why did your parents choose your name?

_____

_____

What is your birth date?

_____

Where were you born? _____

Do you have any brothers or sisters? If so, write
their names below.

_____

_____

Now you are going to write a poem about yourself!

First, read the sample poem about "Grandpop."

Grandpop
Tender, gentle, strong
Someone to hold me
When things go wrong.

Now, you try it.

Write your name:

_____

Write 3 words to describe **you**.
    ("Tender,   gentle,   **strong**")

_____   _____   _____

Write something about **you** on two lines.
("Someone to hold me
When things go **wrong**.")

_____

_____

(Hint: The last word in the last line should
rhyme with the last word in the second line.)

Congratulations on your fine poem!

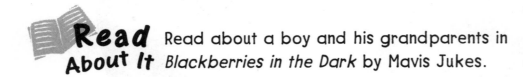

**Read
About It** Read about a boy and his grandparents in
Blackberries in the Dark by Mavis Jukes.

Now, turn the page and get someone in your family to help you. You will be finding out about the members of your family and making a "family tree." A family tree shows where you fit into your family.

Fill in as much of the family tree as you can. Start with your name, birthday, and place of birth. Next, fill in the names of your parents. Add their birthdays and places of birth.

Do as much as you can for your <u>four</u> grandparents and <u>eight</u> great-grandparents. You have now started your family tree!

A Family Tree
Your 8 Great-Grandparents

Name:

Birth Date:

Birthplace:

Name:

Birth Date:

Birthplace:

Name:

Birth Date:

Birthplace:

Name:

Birth Date:

Birthplace:

Your 4 Grandparents

Name:

Birth Date:

Birthplace:

Name:

Birth Date:

Birthplace:

Name:

Birth Date:

Birthplace:

MOM

Name:

YOU

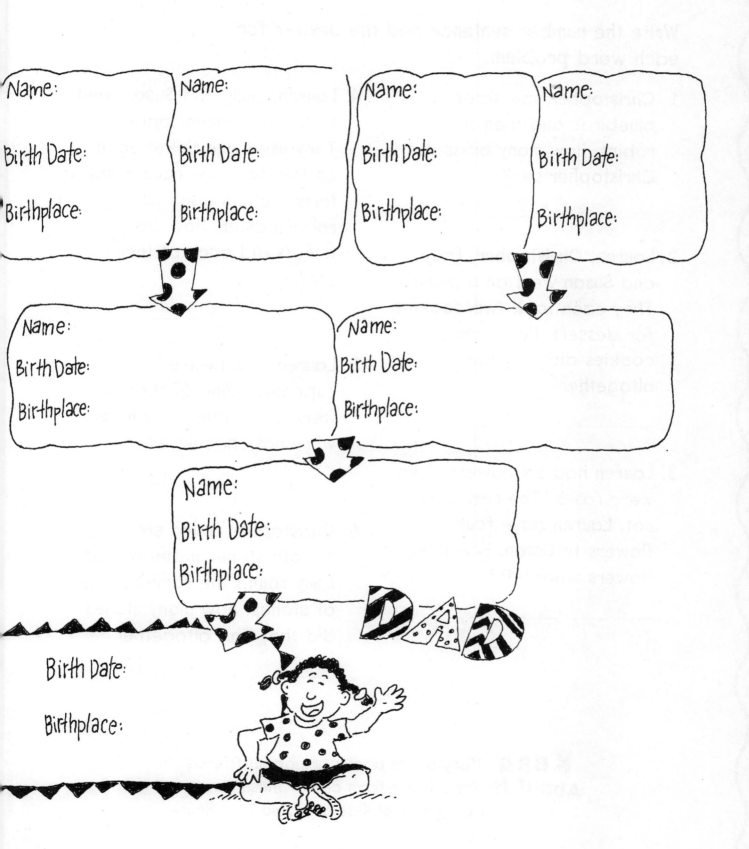

Name:

Birth Date:

Birthplace:

Name:

Birth Date:

Birthplace:

Name:

Birth Date:

Birthplace:

Name:

Birth Date:

Birthplace:

Name:

Birth Date:

Birthplace:

Name:

Birth Date:

Birthplace:

Name:

Birth Date:

Birthplace:

Birth Date:

Birthplace:

DAD

Buddies

Write the **number sentence** and the **answer** for each word problem.

1. **Christopher** saw three bluebirds and then six robins. How many birds did **Christopher** see?

   ___3 + 6 = 9___

2. **Lauren, Christopher, Emily** and **Susan** went on a picnic. They each took two cookies for dessert. How many cookies did they have altogether?

   _____

3. **Lauren** had six flowers. Two were roses. The rest were not. **Lauren** gave four flowers to **Susan.** How many flowers were left?

   _____

4. **Lauren, Emily** and **Susan** went to the amusement park. They used one ticket each on the merry-go-round and three tickets each on the rollercoaster. How many tickets did **each** of them use?

   _____

5. **Lauren** had twelve cupcakes. Nine of them were chocolate. How many were not chocolate?

   _____

6. **Christopher** found six smooth stones in the woods. **Emily** found the same number of stones. How many stones did they find altogether?

   _____

 **Read About It** Many series books are about friends. Try a book from one of these series: Bailey School Kids or Magic Tree House.

Write true or false in front of each of these sentences.

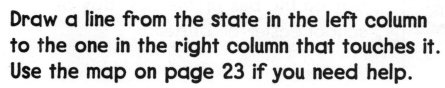

_____ **1.** Earth is the only planet in the solar system.

_____ **2.** A city is smaller than a state.

_____ **3.** The United States is made up of fifty states.

_____ **4.** All states in the United States have the same kind of weather.

Draw a line from the state in the left column to the one in the right column that touches it. Use the map on page 23 if you need help.

California	Florida
Nebraska	Nevada
Alabama	Kansas
Pennsylvania	Ohio

Draw a line through the word that does not belong in each row.

1. Pennsylvania   Florida   Texas   California   Pottstown

2. avenue   state   road   street   drive

3. Jupiter   moon   Mars   Saturn   Uranus   Venus

4. Mexico   England   Japan   Iowa   Brazil   China

Who's Afraid ?

Sometimes children who are going to start kindergarten are scared.

Do you remember being scared when you started kindergarten? Did you ride a bus? Was it scary the first time?

Write a letter to a kindergarten child who might be afraid of starting school. Tell the child what will make the first day on the bus or the first day at school easier or better.

Dear Kindergartener,

_____

_____

_____

_____

_____

_____

_____

_____

Sincerely,

_____

Your name

You Can Count on It!

1. Count by hundreds to 1000.

100, ——, ——, ——, ——, ——, ——, ——, ——, 1000

2. Count by fifties to 1000.

50, 100, 150, ——, ——, ——, ——, 400, ——,

——, ——, ——, ——, ——, ——, ——, ——,

——, 950, ——

3. Count by tens to 105.

5, 15, 25, ——, ——, ——, ——, ——, ——,

——, 105

4. Count by tens from 101 to 201.

101, 111, 121, ——, ——, ——, ——, ——, ——,

——, 201

Rewrite these sentences correctly. Make sure that you use capital letters and periods!

1. when i do my math homework i like to sat at my desk

_____

_____

2. if you ad tin an tin you git twenty

_____

_____

Days, Weeks, and Months

Get a calendar to help you with these questions.

How many

1. days in a year? _____

2. weeks in a month? _____

3. weeks in a year? _____

4. months in a year? _____

Which month has

5. the first day of summer? _____

6. the first day of winter? _____

7. the first day of spring? _____

8. the first day of fall? _____

Read this poem about the months:

Thirty days have September,
April, June, and November;
All the rest have thirty-one,
Excepting—you know which one!

by Anonymous
(that means no one knows who wrote it!)

14

1. Which month does not have 30 or 31 days? _____

2. How many days does that short month have? _____

3. Who wrote the poem on page 14? _____

4. Which months have 30 days?

   _____ , _____ ,

   _____ , and _____

5. Which months have 31 days?

   _____ , _____ ,

   _____ , _____ ,

   _____ , _____ and

   _____ .

6. Write the months of the year in order.

   _____

   _____

   _____

   _____

   _____

   _____

   _____

   _____

   _____

   _____

7. Write the days of the week in order.

   _____

   _____

   _____

   _____

   _____

   _____

   _____

Which month has

1. Halloween? _____
2. the first day of school? _____
3. Valentine's Day? _____
4. Thanksgiving? _____
5. Memorial Day? _____
6. your birthday? _____
7. New Year's Eve? _____
8. New Year's Day? _____
9. the last day of school? _____
10. Washington's birthday? _____
11. St. Patrick's Day? _____
12. Independence Day? _____

Find the word in the box that means the opposite of each numbered word. Write the word's opposite on each line.

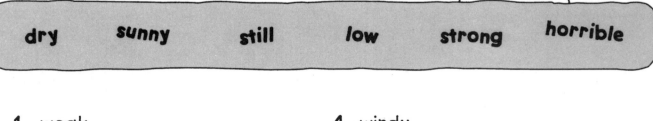

dry   sunny   still   low   strong   horrible

1. weak _____
2. humid _____
3. high _____

4. windy _____
5. cloudy _____
6. lovely _____

Odd or Even?

Write the answer to each question. Then write whether the answer is an __odd__ number or an __even__ number.

1. number of socks in a pair 2/even
2. days in a week _____
3. donuts in a dozen _____
4. years in a decade _____
5. seasons in a year _____
6. planets in our solar system _____
7. states in the U.S.A. _____
8. months in a year _____
9. inches in a foot _____
10. cards in a deck _____
11. letters in the alphabet _____
12. minutes in an hour _____
13. pennies in a quarter _____
14. days in a year _____
15. seconds in a minute _____

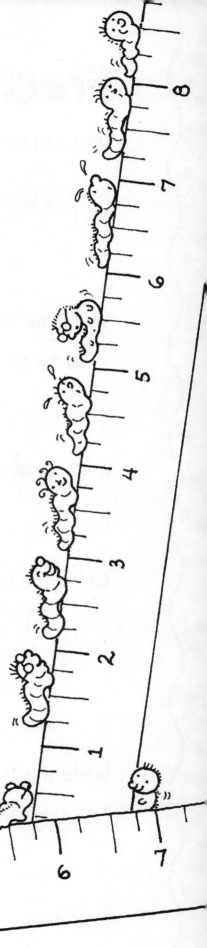

17

Fractions

Do you know these facts about fractions?

A fraction is a part of something.

A fraction is written $\frac{3}{4}$.
You read this as three-fourths.

Write the fraction for the shaded part of the group.

1.

$\frac{2}{5}$

2.

_____

3.

_____

4.

_____

5.

_____

6.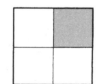

_____

Color the box to show the fraction.

7.

$\frac{3}{4}$

8.

$\frac{1}{6}$

9.

$\frac{5}{12}$

Write the fraction for the shaded part.

10.

_____

11.

_____

12.

_____

Thousands, Hundreds, Tens, Ones

Write as a number.

1. 7 hundreds 2 tens 9 ones _____

2. 3 thousands 4 hundreds 8 tens 2 ones _____

3. 7 hundreds 6 tens 0 ones _____

4. 4 tens 7 ones _____

5. 9 hundreds 0 tens 8 ones _____

6. 8 hundreds 5 tens 8 ones _____

Write the value of the underlined digit in each number.

7. 7 2 **6**   _6 ones_ _____

8. **8** 4 9   _____

9. 5 **0**   _____

10. 4 2 **7**   _____

11. 2 **0** 5   _____

12. **9** 6 1 2   _____

13. The Falcons had a pie eating contest. They ate 14 pies. How many tens and how many ones did they eat?

_____ tens _____ ones

14. A year has 365 days. How many hundreds, tens, and ones are in a year?

_____ hundreds _____ tens _____ ones

Write > or <.

1. 526 _____ 536
2. 7429 _____ 7528
3. 59 _____ 47
4. 767 _____ 676
5. 69 _____ 70
6. 6835 _____ 5832

Write the numbers that come just before and just after.

1. _____ 99 _____
2. _____ 333 _____
3. _____ 8010 _____
4. _____ 790 _____
5. _____ 51 _____
6. _____ 500 _____

Write these numbers in order from least to greatest.

1. 68, 45, 78, 67, 33, 54

   _____

2. 267, 855, 376, 847, 682, 841

   _____

3. 2895, 1365, 4507, 3978, 4498

   _____

Write the underlined word as a number.

1. During July, the Brown family ate forty-six ears of corn.

   _____

2. Randy and his sister climbed one thousand three hundred fifteen feet up Mt. Laurel.

   _____

BRAIN BUSTERS

Lauren and her friend have the same number of coins. Lauren has all dimes. Her friend has all quarters.

Who has more money? _____

20

Our United States

The letters U.S.A. stand for our country— the United States of America. Our country was born in 1776 with the Declaration of Independence.

The United States is made up of 50 states plus a special district called the District of Columbia. The capital, Washington, D.C., is in this district.

1. How many states does our country have? _____

2. What do the letters U.S.A. stand for? _____

_____

3. In what state is the capital found? (careful: this is a trick.)

_____

4. In what year was our country born? _____

Bonus question:
How old is our country today?

_____

The United States is bordered on the east by the Atlantic Ocean and on the west by the Pacific Ocean. Land that touches an ocean is called the coast.

Use the map on page 23 to help you with these questions.

1. What ocean touches the west coast?

_____

2. Name a state that is located on the west coast.

_____

3. What is the name of the ocean that touches the east coast?

_____

4. Name a state that is located on the east coast.

_____

5. Which coast is closer to the state where you live?

_____

6. Other than Alaska, which state is the largest?

_____

7. Which state is the smallest?

_____

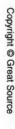

The United States of America

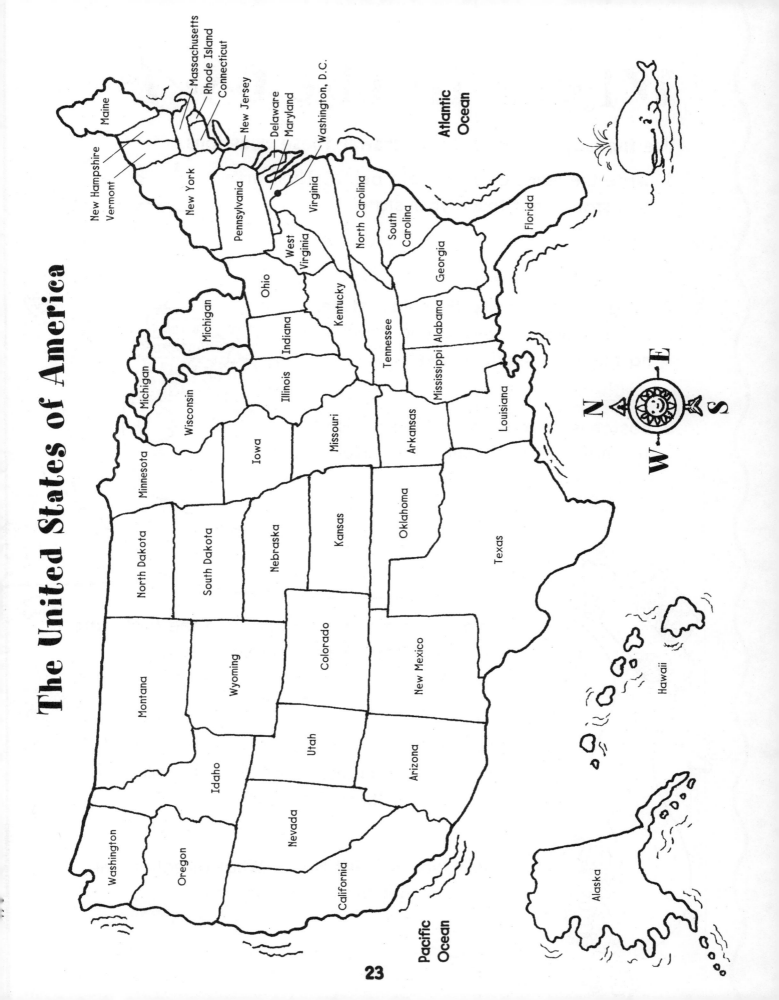

Maine
New Hampshire
Vermont
Massachusetts
Rhode Island
Connecticut
New York
New Jersey
Pennsylvania
Delaware
Maryland
Washington, D.C.
Virginia
West Virginia
North Carolina
South Carolina
Georgia
Florida
Ohio
Kentucky
Tennessee
Alabama
Mississippi
Michigan
Michigan
Wisconsin
Minnesota
Indiana
Illinois
Iowa
Missouri
Arkansas
Louisiana
North Dakota
South Dakota
Nebraska
Kansas
Oklahoma
Texas
Montana
Wyoming
Colorado
New Mexico
Idaho
Utah
Arizona
Washington
Oregon
Nevada
California
Hawaii
Alaska

Atlantic Ocean

Pacific Ocean

N
E
S
W

Where in the USA?

Use the map on page 23 to answer these questions.

1. Write the name of your state below. Then write two states that touch your state.

   _____

   _____

2. To get to California from your state, in what direction would you travel— north, south, east, or west?

   _____

3. Boston is the capital of Massachusetts. In what direction would you travel from your state capital to Boston?

   _____

4. If you start a trip in Missouri and the first state you visit is Utah, what direction would you travel to get there— north, south, east or west?

   _____

5. Now that you are in Utah, your next state to visit will be Montana. What direction will you travel to get there from Utah?

   _____

6. Finally, you will visit Maine. What direction will you go to get there from Montana?

   _____

Telling Time

Answer these questions about time.

1. The big hand on a clock is called the _____ hand.

2. The little hand on a clock is called the _____ hand

3. There are _____ minutes in an hour.

4. How long does it take for the hour hand to move from 4 to 5?

   _____ minutes or _____ hour

Write the correct time below each clock.

5. _____   _____   _____   _____

6. _____   _____   _____   _____

Equal Sums

Circle the numbers that equal the sum at the top of the column.

13	14	15	16
(9 + 4)	7 + 6	8 + 7	8 + 5
8 + 6	9 + 5	9 + 4	9 + 7
5 + 9	5 + 8	6 + 7	8 + 7
2 + 11	9 + 6	5 + 10	7 + 7
6 + 7	6 + 8	9 + 9	4 + 13
7 + 12	3 + 11	7 + 9	8 + 8
9 + 8	4 + 8	9 + 6	7 + 11
8 + 5	7 + 7	4 + 9	9 + 9
4 + 10	7 + 8	6 + 8	8 + 5
9 + 9	5 + 9	7 + 6	7 + 9
4 + 9	8 + 6	6 + 9	9 + 6

JOKE CORNER

A man fell off a 100-foot ladder and wasn't even hurt? Why not?

Answer on page 67.

The Colonies

When the United States was first born, there were only 13 colonies.

Massachusetts

New Hampshire

Pennsylvania

Maryland

Connecticut

New York

Delaware

North Carolina

Rhode Island

New Jersey

Virginia

South Carolina

Georgia

Put the country's 13 colonies in alphabetical order.

1. _____

2. _____

3. _____

4. _____

5. _____

6. _____

7. _____

8. _____

9. _____

10. _____

11. _____

12. _____

13. _____

Elementary School

The best thing about my **elementary school** is

_____

_____

_____

The hardest thing about **second grade** was

_____

_____

_____

When I saw **my teacher** in the morning, I felt

_____

_____

_____

If I could change one thing about **my school,** it would be

_____

_____

_____

JOKE CORNER

What did one wall say to the other?
Answer on page 58.

Money Matters

Get some coins. Make a coin packet using lots of quarters, dimes, nickels, and pennies. You can use your coin packet to help you with the money problems in this book.

Fill in the blanks with the correct amount.

1. $1.00 = _____ dimes
   $1.00 = _____ pennies
   $1.00 = _____ quarters
   $1.00 = _____ nickels

2. $ .50 = _____ dimes
   $ .50 = _____ pennies
   $ .50 = _____ quarters
   $ .50 = _____ nickels

3. 3 nickels = _____ ¢   14 pennies = _____ ¢   4 quarters = _____ ¢

4. 2 quarters = _____ ¢   3 quarters = _____ ¢   7 pennies = _____ ¢

5. 4 dimes = _____ ¢   5 nickels = _____ ¢   6 dimes = _____ ¢

6. $ .25   = _____ quarter
   $ .25 = _____ dimes and _____ nickel
   $ .25 = _____ nickels
   $ .25 = _____ pennies

7. $ .10 = _____ dime
   $ .10 = _____ pennies
   $ .10 = _____ nickels

8. $ .05 = _____ nickel
   $ .05 = _____ pennies

 **Read About It** A girl, her mother, and her grandmother save enough money to buy a special present in *A Chair for My Mother* by Vera B. Williams.

Music

There are many kinds of musical instruments.

__Stringed instruments__ are instruments with strings, like guitars, harps, banjos, and violins.

__Percussion instruments__ are instruments that you hit, like drums, bells, and cymbals.

__Keyboard instruments__ have keys, like the piano and organ.

__Wind instruments__ are instruments you blow into, like the flute, tuba, and trumpet.

In the first blank under the instrument, write the name of the instrument - drum, piano, trumpet, saxophone, violin, French horn, clarinet, or harp.

In the second blank under the instrument, write the kind of instrument - stringed, percussion, keyboard or wind.

1. <u>piano</u>

2. _____

_____

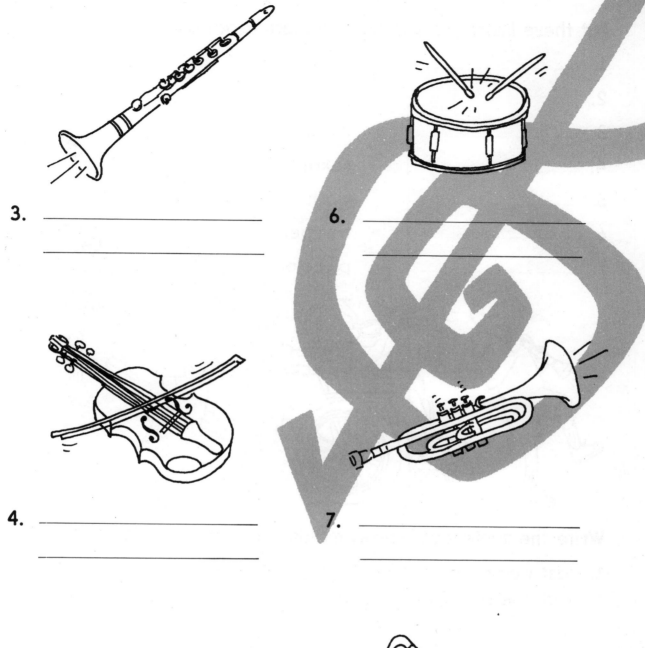

3. _____
   _____

6. _____
   _____

4. _____
   _____

7. _____
   _____

5. _____
   _____

8. _____
   _____

Put these instruments in alphabetical (abc) order.

1. _____   drum

2. _____   piano

3. _____   trombone

4. _____   saxophone

5. _____   violin

6. _____   trumpet

7. _____   piccolo

Write the sentences below, making the corrections.

1. last weak i went to a concert and fel in luv
   with the sound of the small flute called a piccolo

   _____

   _____

2. are school band one the music contest

   _____

   _____

3. did you no that some instruments are made
   from beautiful would

   _____

   _____

My Travels

Draw or paste a picture in the box of a special place you have visited or a place you would like to visit.

Tell why this place is so special to you and what you did when you went there. If you have not been there, tell what you would do if you were to go there.

_____

_____

_____

_____

_____

Calendar Fun

Use the calendar on the next page to answer these questions.

1. On what day of the week is the first day of September?

   _____

2. What date is the third Tuesday of September?

   _____

3. At what time on Wednesdays does Ashley have ballet?

   _____

4. Which comes first, Dad's birthday or Ashley's birthday?

   _____

5. On what day, date, and time
   . . . does Tom have a dentist appointment?

   _____

   . . . does the family have dinner with the grandparents?

   _____

   . . . does school start?

   _____

6. How many full weeks does September have?

   _____

7. On how many mornings in September does
   Mom have 9:00 business meetings?

   _____

HAP
BIRTH

34

Just the Facts, Please

Write number sentences for each fact family.

1.

3	8	11
3 + 8 = 11		
8 + 3 = 11		
11 - 3 = 8		
11 - 8 = 3		

2.

6	7	13

3.

5	4	9

4.

8	6	14

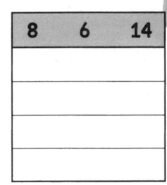

Circle the 3 numbers that make a fact family.
Write the number sentences for each fact family.

5.   15   4   7   2   8

6.   12   7   6   3   5

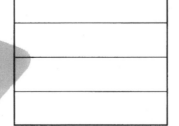

7. Write as many number sentences as you can for the number 16. Several have been done to get you started.

8 + 8 = 16		
17 - 1 = 16		
16 + 0 = 16		

8. Write the sum or difference. Then circle the number sentences that name the number in the box.

5 + 4 + 8 = _____

6 + 9 = _____

19 - 2 = _____

17

9 + 4 + 4 = _____

12 + 5 = _____

10 + 3 + 5 = _____

JOKE CORNER

What has arms and legs but no head?

Answer on page 68.

Continents

Continents are large masses of land on the earth. There are seven continents on earth. The bar graph below compares the size of the continents. Use the graph to complete pages 38 and 39.

Write the continents in alphabetical order.

1. _____
2. _____
3. _____
4. _____
5. _____
6. _____
7. _____

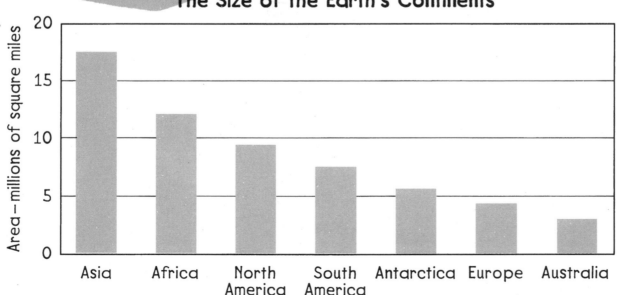

The Size of the Earth's Continents

Area—millions of square miles: 0, 5, 10, 15, 20

Asia | Africa | North America | South America | Antarctica | Europe | Australia

1. Which continent is the largest? _____

2. Which continent is the smallest? _____

3. Which two continents added together almost equal the size of Asia? There can be more than 1 correct answer!

_____ and _____

4. On which continent do you live? _____

5. On which continent might you find

giraffes? _____

kangaroos? _____

penguins? _____

In how many different orders can you put the words earth, sky, and water? Here are two ways:

1. _____ earth _____   _____ sky _____   _____ water _____

2. _____ sky _____   _____ earth _____   _____ water _____

Now, write these three words in as many other orders as you can.

3. _____ _____ _____

4. _____ _____ _____

5. _____ _____ _____

6. _____ _____ _____

Dollars and Cents

Fill in the blank with >, <, or =. You can use coins to help you.

1. 2 nickels __<__ 2 dimes
2. 3 dimes ___ 6 nickels
3. 2 dimes ___ 12 pennies
4. 1 dollar ___ 3 quarters

5. 1 quarter ___ 15 pennies
6. 6 dimes ___ 8 nickels
7. 5 nickels ___ 1 quarter
8. 3 quarters ___ 2 half-dollars

How would you make each amount using as few coins as possible?

Amount	dollars	half-dollars	quarters	dimes	nickels	pennies
$ .45			1	2		
$ .53						
$ .65						
$ .71						
$ .80						
$ .34						
$ .40						
$ .13						
$1.24						
$ .17						

Read About It If you wonder how much a million, a billion, and a trillion is, find out in *How Much Is a Million?* by David Schwartz.

Ancient Troy

Ask your mom, your dad, or a partner to read this story with you.

Over 3000 years ago there was a great city called Troy. It was located in the land that today we call Turkey.

Troy had a wall around it to protect it from enemies. The only way to get into the city of Troy was to go through gates. The gates were guarded by soldiers. The king of Troy was King Priam.

Across the Aegean Sea lived another group of people in a Greek kingdom called Sparta. The king of the Greek kingdom of Sparta was King Menelaus.

The Greeks and the Trojans (the people of Troy) were enemies. The Trojans captured King Menelaus' wife, Helen. Helen was the most beautiful woman in the world. The Greeks sailed to Troy to get Helen back.

A battle took place on the rocky fields outside the gates of Troy. Wagons pulled by horses, called chariots, raced around the battlefield. Spears flew. Many were killed or wounded. Each night the Trojans returned to their walled city. The Greeks camped outside the city of Troy. The war continued for ten years. After ten years, no one had won!

Finally, a Greek leader, Odysseus, had a plan. Odysseus had the Greeks build a huge horse. Many of the Greek soldiers climbed inside the belly of the horse, taking their weapons. The rest of the Greek soldiers pretended to sail home.

The Trojans opened their gates and came outside to celebrate. They looked at the huge wooden horse. They could not believe their eyes. They examined the horse. They decided to bring the horse into their city of Troy. They tied ropes on the horse and dragged it through the gates into their city. They locked the gates with the Trojan horse inside their city.

That night, when all the Trojans were asleep, the Greek soldiers crawled out of the horse. The Greek soldiers who had pretended to sail home came back to Troy. The city of Troy was set on fire and was destroyed. After ten years of fighting, Helen was finally returned home.

Because of the work of archaeologists who discovered the city of Troy, we know that Troy was real. No one has ever found the Trojan horse, however. But it is one of the most famous stories in the world. It was made famous by Homer, a Greek poet who wrote the story of the Trojan War in his poem the *Iliad*.

Across
1. Opposite of "stop"
3. The animal made by the Greeks
4. Wagons pulled by horses
7. What the Trojan horse was made from
8. The King of Sparta

Down
1. What you went through to get into Troy
2. The king of Troy
5. The walled city
7. What surrounded Troy
6. The poet who wrote about the Trojan War

Find That Pattern

Complete the patterns.

1. 5, 10, 15, 20, _____, _____, _____, _____

2. 1, 3, 5, 7, _____, _____, _____, _____

3. 3, 6, 9, 12, _____, _____, _____, _____

4. 1, 5, 9, 13, _____, _____, _____, _____

5. 1, 1, 1, 2, 1, 3, 1, 4, 1, _____, _____, _____,
_____, _____

6. A, B, A, B, C, A, B, C, D, A, B, C, _____, _____, _____,
_____, _____, _____, _____, _____

7. 1, 10, 2, 20, 3, 30, _____, _____, _____, _____,
_____, _____

8. 1, 5, 2, 10, 3, 15, 4, _____, _____, _____,
_____, _____

9. 40, 35, 30, 25, _____, _____, _____, _____, _____

10. A, B, A, C, A, D, A, _____, _____, _____, _____, _____

11. A, Z, A, Y, A, X, A, W, _____, _____, _____, _____,

_____, _____

12. Abby, Bruce, Cathy, David, _____, _____,

_____, _____, _____,

13. 2, 22, 3, 33, 4, 44, _____, _____, _____, _____,

_____, _____

14. 20, 18, 16, 14, _____, _____, _____, _____,

_____,

BRAIN BUSTERS

Now, make up a pattern and see if a family
member or friend can continue your pattern!

_____, _____, _____, _____, _____, _____

_____, _____, _____, _____, _____,

Fraction Shapes

You will need crayons to answer these questions about fractions.

1. Color one-fourth of the shape green.
   Color two-fourths of the shape blue.
   How much of the shape is not colored?

   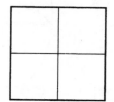

   _____

2. Color two-sevenths of the group blue.
   Color three-sevenths of the group black.
   How much of the group is not colored?

   _____

3. Color two-eighths of the shape red.
   Color three-eighths of the shape blue.
   How much of the shape is not colored?

   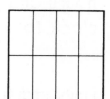

   _____

4. Color 17 squares to make an H.

   Color 12 squares to make an I.

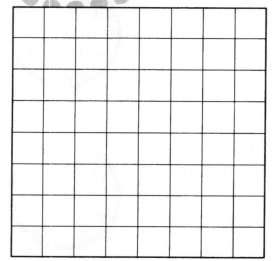

It's Your Birthday!

Pretend that today is your birthday and that you are having a roller-skating party.

1. The party started at 11:15. It lasted two hours and 15 minutes. Draw hands on the clock to show what time the party stopped.

2. Emily started to skate at noon and skated for 25 minutes. Draw hands on the clock to show what time Emily stopped skating.

3. The cake and ice cream were served at 1:00. Everybody finished eating in 25 minutes. Draw hands on the clock to show what time they finished.

4. The next day, the Crane family started their vacation. They started driving at 8:15 in the morning. They drove for 4 hours and then stopped for lunch. Draw hands on the clock to show what time they stopped for lunch.

Gone Fishing

Have you ever really thought about fish? You see them in lakes or fish tanks, but did you ever stop to think how fish are able to live in water?

Both fish and people breathe oxygen. Oxygen is a gas that supports life. Almost all living things need oxygen to live.

Fish get the oxygen they need from water. People get oxygen from the air they breathe.

Lungs

A fish out of water will soon die because it cannot get the oxygen it needs from air.

People get oxygen through their lungs. People have two lungs, which take up most of the room in their chests. People take oxygen into their lungs through their mouths or noses. Fish do not have lungs. Instead, fish use gills, which are located on either side of their heads, to breathe.

When a fish breathes, it takes water in through its mouth. The water then flows through the fish's gills where oxygen is taken out. Next, the water passes out of the fish's body through the openings on either side of its head.

Gill

Like people, fish need sleep. But unlike people, they have no eyelids so they do not close their eyes when sleeping. When fish sleep, they stop swimming and rest. Sometimes they lie on their sides at the bottom of the pond or lake.

Circle the meaning of the underlined word.

1. Both fish and people need <u>oxygen</u> to breathe.

    a plant   a gas that supports life   a lung

2. People get oxygen through their <u>lungs</u>.

    fish   food   part of a person's body

3. Fish use <u>gills</u> to breathe.

    part of a fish's body   air   bones

Circle the correct answer.

1. Fish need oxygen to breathe.   True   False

2. People get oxygen from air.   True   False

3. People and fish have lungs.   True   False

4. Fish can live out of water.   True   False

5. Fish use gills to breathe.   True   False

6. Fish do not need to sleep.   True   False

7. Fish have no eyelids.   True   False

8. Fish close their eyes when they sleep.   True   False

 **Read About It** A boy catches more than he bargains for when he goes fishing in *A Million Fish...More or Less* by Patricia McKissack.

Ready to Multiply

Multiplication is the same as adding the same number again and again. For example,

2 + 2 + 2 + 2 + 2 is the same as 5 x 2.

Solve by adding and then by multiplying.

1. 3 + 3 = _____   2 x 3 = _____

2. 3 + 3 + 3 = _____   3 x 3 = _____

3. 3 + 3 + 3 + 3 = _____   4 x 3 = _____

4. 3 + 3 + 3 + 3 + 3 = _____   5 x 3 = _____

5. 3 + 3 + 3 + 3 + 3 + 3 = _____   6 x 3 = _____

6. 3 + 3 + 3 + 3 + 3 + 3 + 3 = _____   7 x 3 = _____

7. 3 + 3 + 3 + 3 + 3 + 3 + 3 + 3 = _____   8 x 3 = _____

8. 3 + 3 + 3 + 3 + 3 + 3 + 3 + 3 + 3 = _____   9 x 3 = _____

Write these multiplication problems as addition problems. Then solve.

1. 4 x 4 = _____ + _____ + _____ + _____ = _____

2. 4 x 3 = _____ + _____ + _____ + _____ = _____

3. 4 x 2 = _____ + _____ + _____ + _____ = _____

4. 4 x 1 = _____ + _____ + _____ + _____ = _____

5. 2 x 4 = _____ + _____ = _____

6. 2 x 5 = _____ + _____ = _____

 **Read About It** Find out how quickly rice multiplies when you double the amount each day. Read *The King's Chessboard* by David Birch.

Mirror, Mirror, on the Wall

When you look in a mirror, what do you see? You see a reflection of yourself. It looks like you, but everything in your reflection is reversed. What is on your right side appears to be on your reflection's left side.

> **In a mirror, the reflection is always backward.**

Look at the picture above.

1. In which hand is the boy holding the cat?

   _____

2. In which hand is the boy's reflection holding the cat?

   _____

3. Try this yourself. Stand in front of a large mirror. Raise your right hand. Which hand is your reflection raising, the right or the left?

   _____

4. Hold this book up to the mirror and try to read these words.

   SUMMERTIME FUN

   How do the letters look in the mirror?

   _____

You can use mirror writing to write in code or to trick your friends. Try writing your name or a secret message backward so you can read it in the mirror. Hint: Hold your paper up to the mirror and look in the mirror as you write.

Multiplication

Two numbers that are multiplied are called <u>factors</u>.
The answer is called the <u>product</u>.

$$6 \quad X \quad 4 \quad = \quad 24$$

factor   X   factor   =   product

You can use buttons, toothpicks, or some other
counters to help you understand multiplication.
Get 25 counters. Lay them out in sets to help
you find the answer. Here's how you do it.

Here are 3 sets of 4

Here are 4 sets of 5

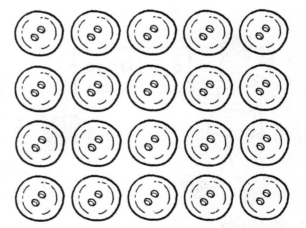

How many buttons are there?

3 sets of 4

$3 \times 4 = 12$

How many buttons are there?

4 sets of 5

$4 \times 5 = 20$

Now you try it. Lay out sets of counters for these multiplication problems. Fill in the answer.

1. 2 x 2 = _____   2. 3 x 3 = _____   3. 2 x 4 = _____

4. 5 x 3 = _____   5. 4 x 4 = _____   6. 2 x 3 = _____

7. 5 x 5 = _____   8. 3 x 4 = _____   9. 4 x 5 = _____

Now use the counters to answer these word problems.

1. Peter has 3 boxes. He has 4 baseball cards in each box. How many baseball cards does he have?

_____ x _____ = _____ cards

2. Hadley has 4 bags of cookies. There are 2 cookies in each bag. How many cookies are there?

_____ x _____ = _____ cookies

3. There are 5 sets of twins at Glenside Elementary School. How many children is that?

_____ x _____ = _____ children

REMEMBER

3 x 4 is the same as 4 x 3

They both equal 12

Multiply.

1. 2 x 3 = _____   2. 4 x 2 = _____   3. 3 x 5 = _____

   3 x 2 = _____   2 x 4 = _____   5 x 3 = _____

4. 5 x 2 = _____   5. 3 x 4 = _____   6. 5 x 4 = _____

   2 x 5 = _____   4 x 3 = _____   4 x 5 = _____

A Fable by Aesop

Once there was a lion who was the great and mighty king of the jungle. One day as the lion lay sleeping in the jungle, a tiny mouse started running up and down on the lion. The lion woke with a start. Stretching out his huge, shaggy paw, he caught the mouse and opened his mouth to eat him.

"Please, please," squeaked the mouse, "do not eat me. If you let me go, one day I may be able to help you out in some way."

This made the lion laugh. The idea that such a tiny, weak creature could help the king of the jungle was very funny indeed. But the lion was kind and he let the mouse go free.

A few days later, the lion was wandering through the jungle. Suddenly he fell into a trap that had been set by hunters. The hunters came and tied the lion to a tree while they went to get a wagon to carry him.

The lion roared for help, but the only creature who dared come near him was the mouse. "Oh, it's just you," sighed the lion. "What can someone so small do to help me?"

"You wait and see," said the mouse as he started chewing at the rope with his sharp little teeth. Before long, the mouse had cut the rope in two and the lion was set free. "Didn't I tell you?" said the mouse. "I may be small but I could help the mighty king of the jungle."

This story was told by a man named Aesop. Aesop was a slave who lived in Greece more than 2500 years ago. He told stories about animals who talk and act like humans. Aesop's stories all have a moral. A moral is a lesson about right and wrong.

Circle the correct answer.

1. The moral of this story is:
   a. You shouldn't believe what people tell you.
   b. It is best to be honest.
   c. Sometimes the small can help the strong.
   d. You should think before you act.

2. What happened last?
   a. The lion fell into the trap.
   b. The mouse ran up and down on the lion.
   c. The mouse chewed the rope in two.
   d. The lion roared for help.

Is it fact or opinion? Write F for fact and O for opinion.

1. _____ This is Aesop's best fable.

2. _____ The mouse was able to help the lion.

3. _____ Lions shouldn't sleep in the jungle.

4. _____ The lion needed help.

5. _____ The hunters weren't very smart.

Circle the meaning of the underlined word in each sentence.

1. The story says that the lion woke with a start. The word <u>start</u> can have two different meanings. In the story, <u>start</u> means

       beginning   jump

2. Once there was a lion who was the great and <u>mighty</u> king of the jungle.

       friendly   hungry   weak   powerful

3. Stretching out his huge, <u>shaggy</u> paw, he caught the mouse and opened his mouth to eat him.

       brown   hairy   beautiful   smooth

4. "Please, please," <u>squeaked</u> the mouse, "do not eat me."

       barked   yelled   peeped   roared

5. The only creature who <u>dared</u> come near him was the mouse.

       was happy to   was brave enough to

Even though you are young and small, you can help your family. Tell how you help people in your family.

_____

_____

_____

_____

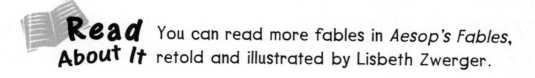

Read About It   You can read more fables in *Aesop's Fables*, retold and illustrated by Lisbeth Zwerger.

Ready to Divide

Get 14 counters. Use them to help you solve these problems.

Jenny went to the beach. She collected 14 seashells. She wants to put them away in boxes with the same number of shells in each box.

1. If Jenny put 2 seashells in each box, how many boxes would she fill? _____ boxes

   How many seashells would be left? _____ seashells

2. If she put 3 seashells in each box, how many boxes would she fill? _____ boxes

   How many seashells would be left? _____ seashells

3. If Jenny put 4 seashells in each box, how many boxes would she fill? _____ boxes

   How many seashells would be left? _____ seashells

4. If she put 5 seashells in each box, how many boxes would she fill? _____ boxes

   How many seashells would be left? _____ seashells

5. If she put 6 seashells in each box, how many boxes would she fill? _____ boxes

   How many seashells would be left? _____ seashells

If I Were President

Write at least 5 sentences to tell what you would do if you were the president of the United States.

_____

_____

_____

_____

_____

_____

_____

_____

_____

_____

_____

_____

_____

_____

_____

_____

_____

Tables

Fill in the table to solve the problems.

1. In the fall, Beth helps her father work in the yard. He pays her $2 each day she helps him. After how many days will she have $12?

_____ days

days	1	2	3			
dollars	$2	$4	$6			

2. Jeff's older sister is on the swim team. She swims 3 miles each day. How many miles will she swim in 6 days?

_____ miles

days						
miles						

3. Hannah's brother gets $5.00 a week for mowing the lawn. How many weeks will it take him to earn $25?

_____ weeks

weeks						
dollars						

Answer from page 28: "Meet me at the corner."

The News

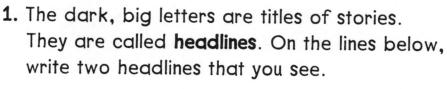

Get your mom or dad or a
partner to help you with this worksheet.
Get a copy of a newspaper. Find the front page.

1. The dark, big letters are titles of stories.
   They are called **headlines**. On the lines below,
   write two headlines that you see.

   _____

   _____

2. The front page has a **table of contents**.
   The table of contents tells you where to find
   something in the newspaper.

3. **Classifieds** are where you find things that
   people are selling. On what page are the
   classifieds?

   Page _____

   Find something for sale in the classifieds.

   What is for sale? _____

   What is the price? _____

   Who do you call or write to? _____

4. **Comics** are sometimes called the "funnies."
   Use the table of contents to find the comics.

   Page _____

5. Go to the comics. See how they are written
   across the page? They are called comic
   "strips." Write the title of one comic strip.

   _____

Pretend that you are writing an article for your school paper about something that happened this summer. It can be about you, someone in your family, or someone in your neighborhood. Write at least 4 good sentences to tell your story about something that happened this summer.

_____
_____
_____
_____
_____
_____
_____
_____

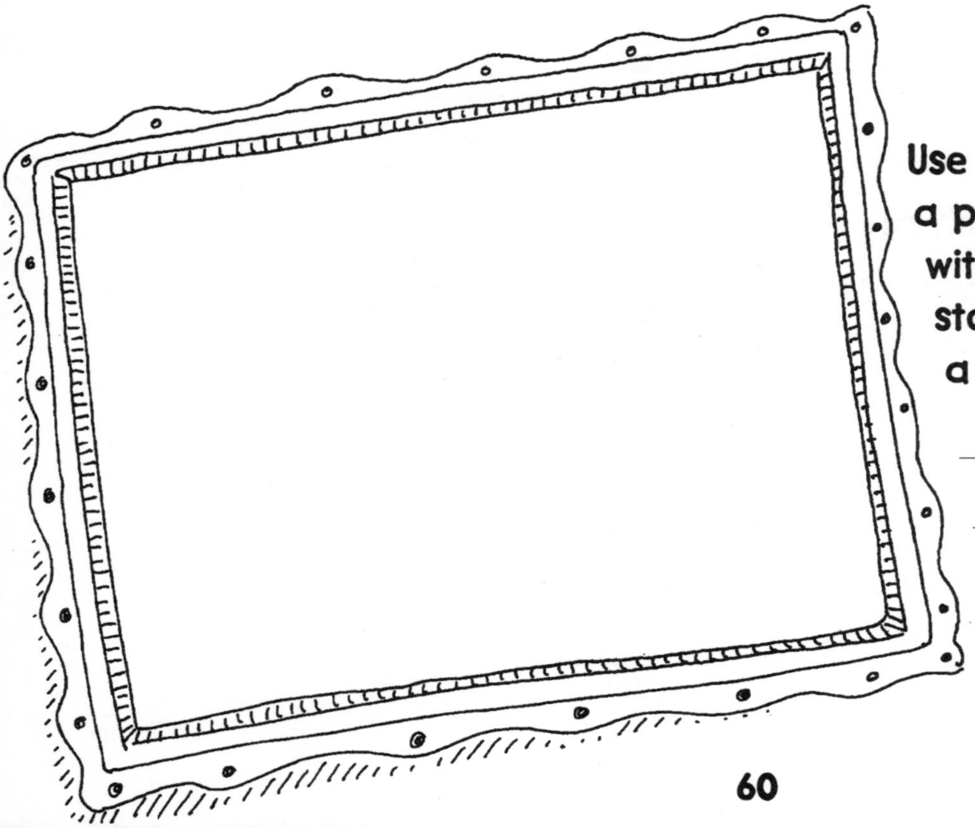

Use this space to draw a picture to go along with your newspaper story. Be sure to write a caption.

_____
_____
_____

An **editorial** is an article in which a writer states an opinion. To prepare to write an editorial, you should first understand both sides of an issue. After you see both sides, then you can decide which side you believe more.

Talk to your partner. Discuss some reasons why students

(i) should have to wear uniforms to school

and

(ii) should not have to wear uniforms to school.

Then, decide which side you agree with more and write an **editorial** answering the following question:

Should students have to wear uniforms to school? Why or why not?

Time Again

Do you know these facts about time?

There are 24 hours in a day.

A.M. means before noon. There are 12 A.M. hours.

P.M. means after noon. There are 12 P.M. hours.

Write the time using A.M. or P.M.

1. 25 minutes after 10 in the morning _____

2. 10 minutes after 8 in the evening _____

3. 55 minutes after 9 at night _____

4. 35 minutes after 7 in the morning _____

Answer these questions about time.

1. It is 3:00 P.M. The movie starts in 25 minutes. What time does the movie start? _____

2. The baseball game started at 8 P.M. It lasted 2 hours and 15 minutes. Was the game held in the morning or at night? _____

3. The swimming meet started at 7:15 P.M. It lasted for 1 hour and 20 minutes. What time did it end? _____

4. Soccer camp started at 8:30 A.M. It lasted for $2\frac{1}{2}$ hours. What time did it end? _____

5. Christopher eats breakfast at 8:00 A.M. He woke up at 7:35 A.M. How long does he have to wait for his breakfast? _____

Fractions and More

Write the fraction for the underlined word.

1. Scott ate <u>two-thirds</u> of a candy bar. _____

2. Kristen made <u>one-sixth</u> of a pot holder. _____

3. Jamie drew a picture on <u>three-fourths</u> of the paper. _____

4. Sarah gave <u>one-half</u> of her popcorn to Jenny. _____

Answer these questions using fractions.

1. Annie had seven stuffed animals. She gave three of them to her friend, Beth. What part did she give to Beth? _____

2. Steven had 5 books. He read 3 of them last week. What part of them did he read last week? _____

3. Andrew's mother ordered a large pizza for dinner. The pizza was cut into 8 pieces. Andrew ate 2 pieces. What fraction of the pizza did he eat? _____

Good Nutrition

You hear a lot about good nutrition. But do you know what this means? Good nutrition is eating enough of the right foods so your body can grow and stay healthy.

There are six main food groups. You need to eat some foods from each of these groups every day to have a healthy diet. Here are the six main food groups and the daily servings you should have from each group. You can also look for the "food pyramid," which is often printed on cereal boxes and other packaged foods.

Food Group	Number of Daily Servings
Fats, oils, sweets	very little
Milk and cheese	2 to 3 servings
Meats and fish	2 to 3 servings
Fruit	2 to 4 servings
Vegetables	3 to 5 servings
Breads and grains	6 to 11 servings

1. From which group do you need to have the most servings?

   _____

2. What is your favorite food in the fruit group? _____

3. Name three foods in the vegetable group.

   _____   _____   _____

4. What food group does ice cream belong to? _____

5. What is your favorite flavor of ice cream? _____

Pretend that this is a list of the foods that you
ate today. Put them in the correct food groups.
Cross them out as you use them.

peaches	chicken	cheese	ham
roll	spaghetti	banana	corn
yogurt	apple	milkshake	tuna fish
peas	cereal	carrots	candy bar

Milk & Cheese	Meats & Fish	Fruit	Vegetables	Breads & Grains	Fats, Oils & Sweets

Now let's find out what you really eat in a day.
Keep a chart of what you ate in one entire day.
Then decide if you ate enough daily servings
from each food group. Count everything you
put into your mouth!

Food	Food Group	Food	Food Group
_____	_____	_____	_____
_____	_____	_____	_____
_____	_____	_____	_____
_____	_____	_____	_____

Now list the total number of servings that you had in each food
group. Did you have enough servings from each food group?

Milk & Cheese	Meats & Fish	Fruit	Vegetables	Breads & Grains	Fats, Oils & Sweets

Money Counts

When counting money, first count the dollars. Then count the coins in this order: half-dollars, quarters, dimes, nickels, pennies.

Each day of the week Great Aunt Jane had a different amount of money in her purse. Add the value of the coins in each row to see how much money she had in her purse on each day. It may be helpful to use coins to do these problems.

Day	dollars	half-dollars	quarters	dimes	nickels	pennies	Total
Sunday		1		5		6	$1.06
Monday	1		2		3		
Tuesday		2	1	3		2	
Wednesday			3	2		1	
Thursday		1	2	1	3	3	
Friday	2		2	3		1	
Saturday	2	1	1	1			

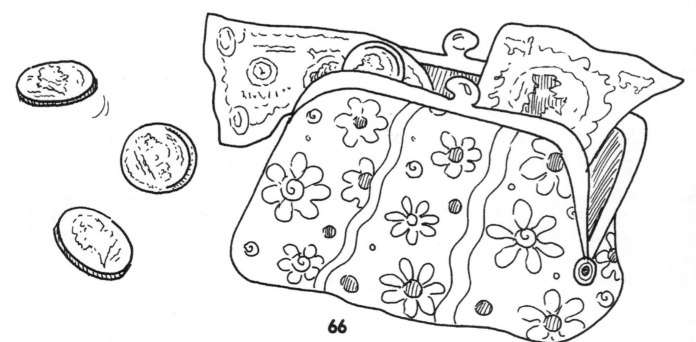

66

1. On what day did Great Aunt Jane have the most money in her purse?

_____

2. On Friday, Great Aunt Jane bought some carrots at the fruit and vegetable stand for $1.50. After she paid for the carrots, how much money did she have in her purse?

_____

3. Did Great Aunt Jane have more money on Tuesday or Thursday?

_____

How much more? _____

4. On Saturday, Great Aunt Jane went to the market to buy some apples. The apples cost $2.50.

Did she have enough money? _____

How much money did she have after she bought the apples?

_____

5. On Monday, Great Aunt Jane found a dime and two pennies on the sidewalk. She put them into her purse. After she added the dime and two pennies, how much money did she have?

_____

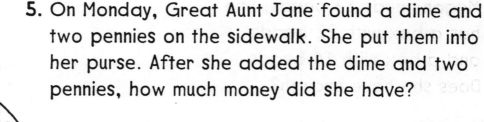

Answer from page 26: He was on the first step.

Math Works

Add or subtract.

1.
49	53	28	64	76
+ 38	+ 14	+ 32	+ 18	+ 9

2.
85	24	92	61	44
− 29	− 13	− 23	− 19	− 35

3.
323	404	276	513	215
+ 38	+ 267	+ 509	+ 347	+ 46

4.
687	459	823	492	743
− 39	− 123	− 604	− 48	− 529

Solve the problems.

Show the number sentences.

1. Megan needs 53 beads. She has a box with 22 beads and a box with 14 beads. Does she have enough?

_____

_____

2. Linda sold 139 tickets in the morning. She sold 242 tickets in the afternoon. How many more tickets did she sell in the afternoon than in the morning?

_____ tickets

_____

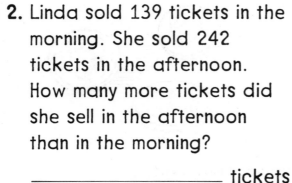

Answer from page 37: A chair

SOUND TRAVELS

Every day we hear many different kinds of sounds: horns blowing, children laughing, a clock ticking, telephones ringing. But how do these sounds travel to our ears?

In order for us to hear sound, there must be something to carry the sound to our ears. Most of the time, sound travels through air. But sound travels through other things as well: metal, wood, water, the ground.

Go outside and have a friend stand about 20 feet from you. Put your ear to the ground as he jumps up and down. Can you hear his jumps through the ground?

Put an alarm clock at the end of a wood table. Put your ear on the table at the other end. Can you hear the clock ticking through the wood?

You and your friend can make a string telephone to carry sound. To do this, you will need:

Two paper cups
20-40 feet of string
Tape Pin

Put a hole in the bottom of each cup with a pin. Push the ends of the string through each cup and tape the ends to the bottoms of the cups. Have your friend walk away from you until the string is pulled tight. Take turns whispering or talking into the cup while the other person listens.

What carries the sound of your voice to your friend's ear?

A Letter to Your Third Grade Teacher

Write a letter to your third grade teacher. Tell at least three interesting facts about yourself that you think your teacher should know.

Dear Third Grade Teacher,

_____

_____

_____

_____

_____

_____

_____

_____

_____

_____

_____

_____

From your new student,

_____

Sign your name here

Book Section

The book section provides worksheets
for seven books. Three are chosen.
The last four are free choice.

A Mare for Young Wolf by Janice Shefelman

Sylvester and the Magic Pebble by William Steig

Dinosaurs Before Dark by Mary Pope Osborne

A Mare for Young Wolf

Read A Mare for Young Wolf by Janice Shefelman.

Circle the best ending to the sentence.

A "mare" is a female horse.

1. Young Wolf named his favorite horse Red Wind because
   a. she ran past him and knocked him over.
   b. she was red and ran like the wind.
   c. she loved to hide in red trees.

2. Eagle Feather was unhappy at first with Young Wolf's choice of horse because
   a. another warrior had already chosen Red Wind.
   b. Red Wind was not strong and healthy.
   c. mares were for children and women.

3. We can guess that Young Wolf
   a. was a sissy because he chose a mare.
   b. was brave to choose the mare even if others thought he should not.
   c. chose a mare because he was afraid of a real horse.

4. The last sentence of chapter 1 says, "Young Wolf's heart lay on the ground." This means
   a. Young Wolf was so sad, it felt as if his heart dropped onto the ground.
   b. someone injured Young Wolf, and his heart fell to the ground.
   c. Young Wolf lay on the ground, and therefore his heart was on the ground.

5. What is Grandfather trying to teach Young Wolf in chapter 2? Grandfather is trying to teach Young Wolf

_____

6. In chapter 2, we are told "Young Wolf's heart was hot." This means

_____

_____

7. In chapter 3, called "Young Wolf's Idea," Young Wolf has an idea about how he can make Red Wind trust him. What is that idea?

_____

8. What was the purpose of the loop Grandfather made for Red Wind?

_____

_____

What was the loop made from?

_____

9. Chapter 4 starts with the sentence, "It was the moon of painted leaves." What season do you think it is?

_____

10. What made Red Wind a hero?

_____

_____

_____

Here are some action words used in *A Mare for Young Wolf*.

| clench | nuzzle | mount | bolt | summon |

1. Which word can mean "to run away suddenly"?

   _____

2. Which word can mean "to snuggle or rub the nose into"?

   _____

3. Which word can mean "to call for someone"?

   _____

4. Which word can mean "to make a fist"?

   _____

5. Which word can mean "to get on top of"?

   _____

Draw a picture of your favorite part of the story.

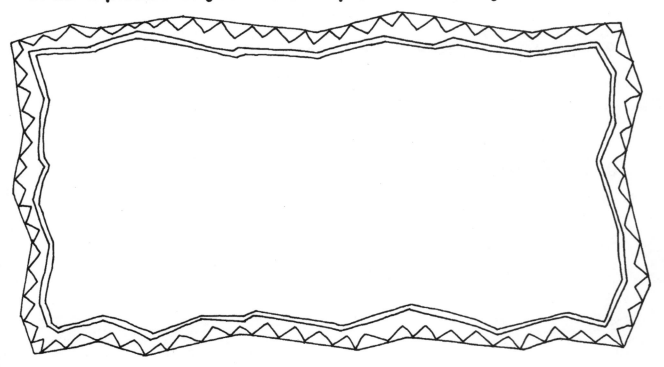

Sylvester and The Magic Pebble

Read *Sylvester and the Magic Pebble*, by William Steig.

Number these sentences 1 through 6 to show the order in which they happened.

———— A lion came, and Sylvester wished he were a rock.

———— Sylvester found a red, shiny pebble.

———— Sylvester wished that he were himself again.

———— Long after Sylvester became a rock, Sylvester's parents had a picnic on Sylvester.

———— Sylvester found that each time he made a wish, so long as he was holding the red pebble, the wish would come true.

———— Sylvester's parents found the red pebble and put it on the rock that was Sylvester.

Unscramble these words to make sentences.
Write the sentences.

1. collected   rocks   unusual   and   Sylvester   pebbles

   _____

2. first   fun   making   Sylvester   At   wishes   had

   _____

3. dogs   All   searched   neighborhood   the   the

   _____

Match the words that mean the same (synonyms).

1. ceased   confused

2. vanished   stopped

3. extraordinary   disappeared

4. perplexed   unusual

In the blanks, write F̲ for fact and O̲ for opinion.

———— 1. Sylvester could have wished that the lion would go away.

———— 2. Sylvester's mother was much more upset than Sylvester's father.

———— 3. Sylvester will never use the pebble foolishly again.

———— 4. Sylvester was very unhappy as a rock.

Circle the meaning of the underlined word.

1. Sylvester found that his wishes were gratified as soon as he made them.

      lost   satisfied   forgotten

2. The lion was bewildered when the donkey disappeared.

   confused   joyful   freezing

     3. Mr. Duncan did his best to soothe Mrs. Duncan.

      bother   tickle   comfort

     4. Sylvester was startled to see the lion.

     surprised   thrilled   sad

At the end of the story, Mr. Duncan put the magic pebble in an iron safe. Pretend that Sylvester lets **you** use the magic pebble for just one wish. What would you wish? Why? Be sure to write at least four complete sentences.

Dinosaurs Before Dark

Get a copy of the first book in the Magic Tree House series called *Dinosaurs Before Dark*. The author is Mary Pope Osborne. Read the book and enjoy it! Then answer the following questions.

1. A **fiction** book tells a make-believe story. A **nonfiction** book tells a true story. Is this book fiction or nonfiction?

   _____

2. How old is Annie?   How old is Jack?

   _____   _____

3. A **compound word** is made up of two words. Find three compound words used in this book. Write them below. (Hint: You will find compound words on pages 2, 6, 7, 12, 13, 29, and 45!)

   _____

   _____

   _____

4. Now, **alphabetize** (put into ABC order) the three compound words that you found and wrote above.

   _____

   _____

   _____

5. The last thing that happened before the dinosaurs appeared was that

   a. Jack and Annie were climbing down the tree to go home.

   b. Jack said, " I wish I could see a Pteranodon for real."

   c. Annie was reading out loud from a book about castles.

6. Jack and Annie traveled to the land of the dinosaurs

   a. in a spinning tree house.

   b. on the back of the Pteranodon.

   c. by car, boat, and then train.

7. Write each group of words in the correct order to make a complete sentence.

   a.   children   rescued   The   by   were   the   Pteranodon

   _____

   b.   found   a   Jack   medallion   ground   on   gold   the

   _____

8. Write <u>F</u> on the line by the sentence that is a fact. Write <u>O</u> by the sentence that is an opinion.

   _____   **a.** Jack and Annie were lucky to see real dinosaurs.

   _____   **b.** Jack found a picture of Frog Creek, Pennsylvania, and wished that he was home.

Jack and Annie saw a Pteranodon, a Triceratops, an Anatosaurus, and a Tyrannosaurus rex. Choose one of these dinosaurs. Write at least three sentences to describe that dinosaur. Then, draw a picture of the dinosaur that you chose.

_____

_____

_____

_____

_____

_____

An author makes a story interesting by painting pictures in the mind of the reader. One way to paint pictures is to use comparisons.

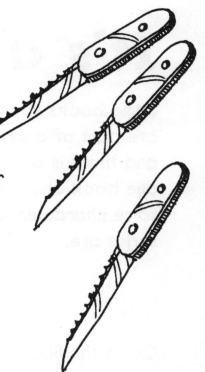

1. The story says that the Tyrannosaurus rex had teeth **"as big as steak knives."**

   You can really picture those teeth! The author could have used <u>many</u> different comparisons. How about teeth **"as big as axe blades"** ? Can you think of another way to describe big, sharp teeth? Try it below.

   The Tyrannosaurus rex's teeth were as big as

   _____.

2. The story says that the Pteranodon looked **"like a glider plane."**

   Can you describe how the big, flying dinosaur looked by making up your own comparison?

   When the Pteranodon flew, it looked like

   _____.

3. Try one more. The story says that when the Tyrannosaurus rex hit the tree house, it **"shook like a leaf."** Make up your own comparison to describe how the tree house shook.

   When hit by the dinosaur, the tree house shook like

   _____.

It's a Series!

Some books you read are part of a series, and there is more than one book about the same character. Some series are:

A series about **Nate the Great,** by Marjorie Weinman Sharmat

A series about **Cam Jansen,** by David Adler

A series called **The Boxcar Children,** by Gertrude Chandler Warner

A series of sports books, by Matt Christopher

A series called **Magic Tree House,** by Mary Pope Osborne

A series about **Jenny Archer,** by Ellen Conford

Go to the library or bookstore and look at these series or any other series you might see. Choose **two** books from **one** of the series. Pick books that you have not already read.

Read the two books, and then complete these questions.

1. What series did you choose?

_____

2. What are the names of the two books that you chose?

   a. _____

   b. _____

3. What characters are in both of your books?

_____

_____

4. Choose the book that you read first, and
answer these questions:

a. What characters were in this book but not in the second book?

_____

b. What is the problem in this book?

_____

_____

_____

c. How is the problem solved?

_____

_____

_____

_____

5. Choose the book that
you read second, and answer these questions:

a. What characters were in this book but not in the first book?

_____

b. What is the problem in this book?

_____

_____

_____

c. How is the problem solved?

_____

_____

_____

6. Which book did you like better?

_____

Why? _____

_____

_____

_____

If you enjoyed your series, read on!

Read another book or two in the series.
Or, try another series. It's fun to get to
know characters who are in several books!

List books in other series that you have read.

_____

_____

_____

_____

Biography

A **biography** is a true story about a real person. That person could have lived long ago or could still be alive. Some biographies are about important leaders of government and business. Some are about famous sports people and movie stars. There are biographies about famous scientists, artists, and musicians. Find a biography that you would like to read. After you read it, answer the questions.

1. What is the name of your book?

   _____

2. Who was your biography about?

   _____

3. Did your biography tell you about the person from the time he or she was born until he or she died? Or, did your biography just tell you about a short time in this person's life?

   _____

4. What made the person in your biography famous?

   _____

   _____

   _____

   _____

   _____

5. Do you think that the author of your biography liked the person in your biography? Why or why not?

_____

_____

_____

6. Did the author of your biography actually know the person he or she wrote about?

_____

_____

_____

7. What was the most interesting fact you learned about the person in your biography?

_____

_____

_____

Draw a picture of the person in your biography.

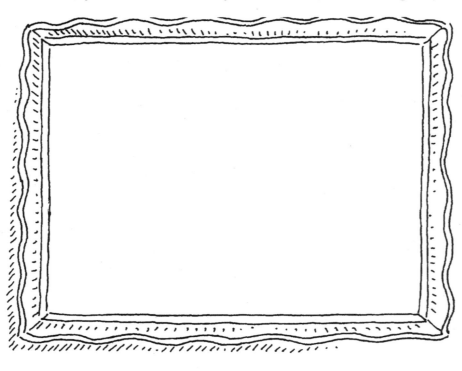

Map Out a Book

Now is your chance to pick any book that you would like to read.

What is the title of your book?

_____

Who is the author of your book?

_____

After you read the book, follow the instructions in the boxes below.

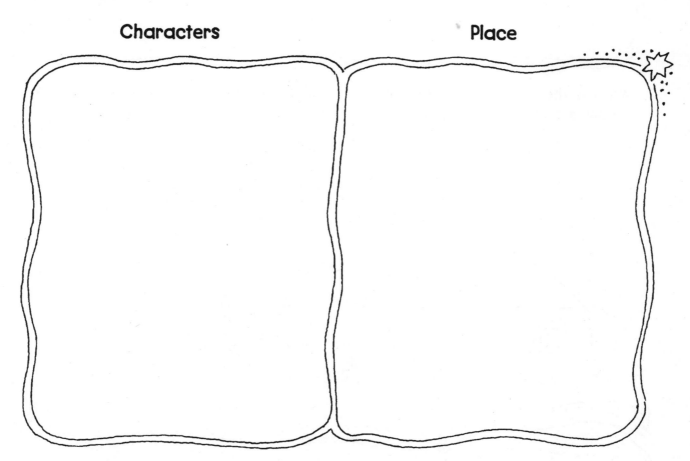

Characters	Place

Who are the characters?
Draw a picture of them.

Where does the story take place?
Draw a picture of the place.

Problem   **Solution**

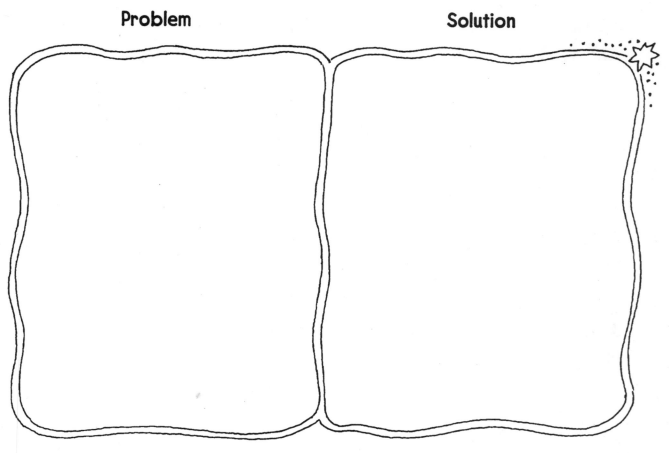

What is the problem in the story?
Draw a picture of the problem.

What is the solution to the problem?
Draw a picture of the solution.

Answer Key

PAGE 6
1. $3 + 6 = 9$
2. $4 \times 2 = 8$
3. $6 - 4 = 2$
4. $1 \times 4 = 4$
5. $12 - 9 = 3$
6. $6 + 6 = 12$

PAGE 7
(Answer chart →)
Brain Buster: 0, 12

0	10	13	16	14	18	15	12
3	7	10	13	11	15	12	9
7	3	6	9	7	11	8	5
9	1	4	7	5	9	6	3
6	4	7	10	8	12	9	6
4	6	9	12	10	14	11	8
8	2	5	8	6	10	7	4
5	5	8	11	9	13	10	7

PAGE 8
1. 10, 20, 30, 40, 50, 60, 70, 80, 90, 100
2. ten, twenty, thirty, forty, fifty, sixty, seventy, eighty, ninety, one hundred
3. eighty-nine, nine hundred seventy-three, thirty-six, five hundred sixty-nine, seventy-one

Brain Buster: Katie

PAGE 9
(Answer chart →)
Brain Buster: 3, Lisa

0	9	2	5	3	8	4	6
7	16	9	12	10	15	11	13
8	17	10	13	11	16	12	14
4	13	6	9	7	12	8	10
3	12	5	8	6	11	7	9
9	18	11	14	12	17	13	15
6	15	8	11	9	14	10	12
5	14	7	10	8	13	9	11

PAGE 10
1.-3. Answers will vary
4. United States of America
5. North America
6. Northern and Western
7. Earth
8. Milky Way

PAGE 11
1. False
2. True
3. True
4. False
5. California—Nevada
6. Nebraska—Kansas
7. Alabama—Florida
8. Pennsylvania—Ohio

1. Pottstown
2. state
3. moon
4. Iowa

PAGE 13
1. 100, 200, 300, 400, 500, 600, 700, 800, 900, 1000
2. 50, 100, 150, 200, 250, 300, 350, 400, 450, 500, 550, 600, 650, 700, 750, 800, 850, 900, 950, 1000
3. 5, 15, 25, 35, 45, 55, 65, 75, 85, 95, 105
4. 101, 111, 121, 131, 141, 151, 161, 171, 181, 191, 201

1. When I do my math homework I like to sit at my desk.
2. If you add ten and ten you get twenty.

PAGE 14
1. 365
2. 4 to 5
3. 52
4. 12
5. June
6. December
7. March
8. September

PAGE 15
1. February
2. 28 or 29
3. Anonymous
4. September, April, June, November
5. January, March, May, July, August, October, December
6. January, February, March, April, May, June, July, August, September, October, November, December
7. Sunday, Monday, Tuesday, Wednesday, Thursday, Friday, Saturday

PAGE 16
1. October
2. Answers will vary
3. February
4. November
5. May
6. Answers will vary
7. December
8. January
9. Answers will vary
10. February
11. March
12. July

1. weak—strong
2. humid—dry
3. high—low
4. windy—still
5. cloudy—sunny
6. lovely—horrible

PAGE 17
1. 2, even
2. 7, odd
3. 12, even
4. 10, even
5. 4, even
6. 9, odd
7. 50, even
8. 12, even
9. 12, even
10. 52 or 54, even
11. 26, even
12. 60, even
13. 25, odd
14. 365, odd
15. 60, even

PAGE 18
2. $\frac{4}{7}$
3. $\frac{7}{10}$
4. $\frac{5}{6}$
5. $\frac{5}{8}$
6. $\frac{7}{12}$
7. (Answer →)
8. (Answer →)
9. (Answer →)
10. $\frac{3}{8}$
11. $\frac{12}{12}$ or 1
12. $\frac{1}{4}$

89

PAGE 19
1. 729
2. 3482
3. 760
4. 47
5. 908
6. 858
7. 6 ones
8. 8 hundreds
9. 0 ones
10. 7 ones
11. 0 tens
12. 9 thousands
13. 1 ten, 4 ones
14. 3 hundreds, 6 tens, 5 ones

PAGE 20
1. <
2. <
3. >
4. >
5. <
6. >

1. 98, 99, 100
2. 332, 333, 334
3. 8009, 8010, 8011
4. 789, 790, 791
5. 50, 51, 52
6. 499, 500, 501

1. 33, 45, 54, 67, 68, 78
2. 267, 376, 682, 841, 847, 855
3. 1365, 2895, 3978, 4498, 4507

1. 46
2. 1315
Brain Buster: Her friend

PAGE 21
1. 50
2. United States of America
3. no state, but a district
4. 1776
Bonus: Answers will vary.

PAGE 22
1. Pacific Ocean
2. Washington, Oregon, or California
3. Atlantic Ocean
4. Maine, New Hampshire, Massachusetts, Rhode Island, Connecticut, New York, New Jersey, Delaware, Maryland, Virginia, North Carolina, South Carolina, Georgia, or Florida
5. Answers will vary.
6. Texas
7. Rhode Island

PAGE 24
1.-3. Answers will vary.
4. west
5. north
6. east or northeast

PAGE 25
1. minute
2. hour
3. 60
4. 60 minutes or 1 hour

5. 11:10, 1:15, 10:45, 1:35
6. 5:20, 6:05, 2:50, 12:40

PAGE 26

13	14	15	16
9 + 4	9 + 5	8 + 7	9 + 7
2 + 11	6 + 8	5 + 10	8 + 8
6 + 7	3 + 11	9 + 6	7 + 9
8 + 5	7 + 7	6 + 9	
4 + 9	5 + 9		
	8 + 6		

PAGE 27
1. Connecticut
2. Delaware
3. Georgia
4. Maryland
5. Massachusetts
6. New Hampshire
7. New Jersey
8. New York
9. North Carolina
10. Pennsylvania
11. Rhode Island
12. South Carolina
13. Virginia

PAGE 29
1. 10 dimes, 100 pennies, 4 quarters, 20 nickels
2. 5 dimes, 50 pennies, 2 quarters, 10 nickels
3. 15¢, 14¢, 100¢ or $1.00
4. 50¢, 75¢, 7¢
5. 40¢, 25¢, 60¢
6. 1 quarter, 2 dimes and 1 nickel, 5 nickels, 25 pennies
7. 1 dime, 10 pennies, 2 nickels
8. 1 nickel, 5 pennies

PAGES 31–32
1. piano, keyboard
2. harp, stringed
3. clarinet, wind
4. violin, stringed
5. French horn, wind
6. drum, percussion
7. trumpet, wind
8. saxophone, wind

PAGE 32
1. drum
2. piano
3. piccolo
4. saxophone
5. trombone
6. trumpet
7. violin

1. Last week I went to a concert and fell in love with the sound of the small flute called a piccolo.
2. Our school band won the music contest.
3. Did you know that some instruments are made from beautiful wood?

PAGE 34
1. Friday
2. September 19
3. 3:30 P.M.
4. Ashley's birthday
5. 12:30 P.M. on Tuesday, September 12; 6:00 P.M. on Monday, September 18; 7:30 A.M. on Thursday, September 7
6. 4
7. 3

PAGES 36–37
2. 6 + 7 = 13, 7 + 6 = 13, 13 - 6 = 7, 13 - 7 = 6
3. 5 + 4 = 9, 4 + 5 = 9, 9 - 5 = 4, 9 - 4 = 5
4. 8 + 6 = 14, 6 + 8 = 14, 14 - 8 = 6, 14 - 6 = 8
5. 8 + 7 = 15, 7 + 8 = 15, 15 - 8 = 7, 15 - 7 = 8
6. 5 + 7 = 12, 7 + 5 = 12, 12 - 5 = 7, 12 - 7 = 5
7. Answers will vary but must equal 16.
8. 5 + 4 + 8 = 17, 19 - 2 = 17, 9 + 4 + 4 = 17, 12 + 5 = 17

PAGE 38
1. Africa
2. Antarctica
3. Asia
4. Australia
5. Europe
6. North America
7. South America

PAGE 39
1. Asia
2. Australia
3. Africa and Antarctica
   North and South America
4. North America
5. Africa, Australia, Antarctica

PAGE 40
1. <
2. =
3. >
4. >
5. >
6. >
7. =
8. <

Amount	dollars	half-dollars	quarters	dimes	nickels	pennies
$ .45			1	2		
$ .53		1				3
$ .65		1		1	1	
$ .71		1		2		1
$ .80		1	1		1	
$ .34			1		1	4
$ .40			1	1	1	
$ .13				1		3
$1.24	1			2		4
$ .17				1	1	2

PAGE 42
Across
1. go
3. horse
4. chariots
7. wood
8. Menelaus

Down
1. gates
2. Priam
5. Troy
6. Homer
7. wall

PAGE 43
1. 5, 10, 15, 20, 25, 30, 35, 40
2. 1, 3, 5, 7, 9, 11, 13, 15
3. 3, 6, 9, 12, 15, 18, 21, 24
4. 1, 5, 9, 13, 17, 21, 25, 29
5. 1, 1, 1, 2, 1, 3, 1, 4, 1, 5, 1, 6, 1, 7
6. A, B, A, B, C, A, B, C, D, A, B, C, D, E, A, B, C, D, E, F
7. 1, 10, 2, 20, 3, 30, 4, 40, 5, 50, 6, 60
8. 1, 5, 2, 10, 3, 15, 4, 20, 5, 25, 6, 30
9. 40, 35, 30, 25, 20, 15, 10, 5, 0
10. A, B, A, C, A, D, A, E, A, F, A, G

11. A, Z, A, Y, A, X, A, W, A, V, A, U, A, T
12. The pattern continues through the alphabet with alternating male and female names.
13. 2, 22, 3, 33, 4, 44, 5, 55, 6, 66, 7, 77
14. 20, 18, 16, 14, 12, 10, 8, 6, 4, 2

PAGE 45
1. $\frac{1}{4}$
2. $\frac{2}{7}$
3. $\frac{3}{8}$

PAGE 46
1. 1:30
2. 12:25
3. 1:25
4. 12:15

PAGE 48
1. a gas that supports life
2. part of a person's body
3. part of a fish's body
1. True   5. True
2. True   6. False
3. False   7. True
4. False   8. False

PAGE 49
1. 6   5. 18
2. 9   6. 21
3. 12   7. 24
4. 15   8. 27

1. 4 + 4 + 4 + 4 = 16
2. 3 + 3 + 3 + 3 = 12
3. 2 + 2 + 2 + 2 = 8
4. 1 + 1 + 1 + 1 = 4
5. 4 + 4 = 8
6. 5 + 5 = 10

PAGE 50
1. right hand
2. left hand
3. left hand
4. backwards

PAGE 52
1. 4   6. 6
2. 9   7. 25
3. 8   8. 12
4. 15   9. 20
5. 16

1. 3 X 4 = 12   3. 5 X 2 = 10
2. 4 X 2 = 8

1. 6   4. 10
2. 8   5. 12
3. 15   6. 20

PAGE 54
1. c   2. c

1. O   4. F
2. F   5. O
3. O

91

PAGE 55
1. jump
2. powerful
3. hairy
4. peeped
5. was brave enough to

PAGE 56
1. 7 boxes, none left
2. 4 boxes, 2 left
3. 3 boxes, 2 left
4. 2 boxes, 4 left
5. 2 boxes, 2 left

PAGE 58
1. 6 days
2. 18 miles
3. 5 weeks

PAGE 62
1. 10:25 A.M.
2. 8:10 P.M.
3. 9:55 P.M.
4. 7:35 A.M.

1. 3:25 P.M.
2. night
3. 8:35 P.M.
4. 11:00 A.M.
5. 25 minutes

PAGE 63
1. $\frac{2}{3}$
2. $\frac{1}{6}$
3. $\frac{3}{4}$
4. $\frac{1}{2}$

1. $\frac{3}{7}$
2. $\frac{3}{5}$
3. $\frac{2}{8}$ or $\frac{1}{4}$

PAGE 64
1. Breads and grains
4. Milk and cheese

PAGE 65

Milk & Cheese	Meats & Fish	Fruit	Vegetables	Breads & Grains	Fats, Oils & Sweets
yogurt	chicken	peaches	peas	roll	candy bar
cheese	ham	apple	carrots	spaghetti	
milkshake	tuna fish	banana	corn	cereal	

PAGE 66
Sunday $1.06
Monday $1.65
Tuesday $1.57
Wednesday $ .96
Thursday $1.28
Friday $2.81
Saturday $2.85

PAGE 67
1. Saturday
2. $1.31 left
3. Tuesday; $ .29
4. yes; $ .35
5. $1.77

PAGE 68
1. 87, 67, 60, 82, 85
2. 56, 11, 69, 42, 9
3. 361, 671, 785, 860, 261
4. 648, 336, 219, 444, 214

1. 22 + 14 = 36; no
2. 242 - 139 = 103

PAGES 72–73
1. b
2. c
3. b
4. a
5. He was teaching Young Wolf to ride Red Wind to make her the best war horse in the village.
6. Young Wolf was very angry.
7. He used Red Wind as a pillow to sleep.
8. The loop was so that Young Wolf could put in his head and arm and ride on the side of Red Wind during battle. The loop was made of horsehair.
9. autumn or fall
10. Red Wind pulled on her rope to warn Young Wolf that the Apaches had invaded the village.

PAGE 74
1. bolt
2. nuzzle
3. summon
4. clench
5. mount

PAGE 75
3, 1, 6, 4, 2, 5
1. Sylvester collected unusual rocks and pebbles.
2. At first Sylvester had fun making wishes.
3. All the dogs searched the neighborhood.

PAGE 76
1. ceased—stopped
2. vanished—disappeared
3. extraordinary—unusual
4. perplexed—confused

1. F
2. O
3. O
4. F

1. satisfied
2. confused
3. comfort
4. surprised

PAGES 78–79
1. fiction
2. Annie is 7. Jack is 8 1/2.
3. Examples include afternoon, everywhere, and bookmarks.
4. The words should be in correct alphabetical order.
5. b
6. a
7. a. The children were rescued by the Pteranodon.
   b. Jack found a gold medallion on the ground.
8. a. O
   b. F